Nita Mehta's

Best of
Indian
Cooking

Nita Mehta's
Best of
Indian Cooking

Nita Mehta

B.Sc. (Home Science), M.Sc. (Food and Nutrition), Gold Medalist

Tanya Mehta

SNAB

Nita Mehta's
Best of
Indian Cooking

First Hardbound Edition 2007

ISBN 978-81-7869-180-0

Food Styling & Photography: Tanya Mehta

Layout and laser typesetting:

National Information Technology Academy
3A/3, Asaf Ali Road
New Delhi-110 002
☎ 23252948

Published by:

SNAB
Publishers Pvt Ltd
3A/3 Asaf Ali Road
New Delhi-110002

The Best of Cookery Books

Editorial and Marketing office:
E-159, Greater Kailash-II, N.Delhi-48
Tel: 91-11-23252948, 23250091, Fax: 91-11-29225218
Tel: 91-11-29214011, 29218727, 29218574
E-Mail: nitamehta@email.com
nitamehta@nitamehta.com
Website: http://www.nitamehta.com
Website: http://www.snabindia.com

Printed at:
STANDARD PRESS (INDIA) PVT. LTD.

Contributing Writers:
Subhash Mehta
Anurag Mehta

Distributed by:
THE VARIETY BOOK DEPOT
A.V.G. Bhavan, M 3 Con Circus
New Delhi - 110 001
Tel: 23417175, 23412567; Fax: 23415335

Editorial & Proofreading:
Ekta
Deepali

Price: Rs. 250/-

Introduction

*T*he true art of Indian cooking lies in the subtle use and variation of spices which make each dish exotic and an exciting new experience. The use of spices, however, does not mean their use in vast amounts, nor does it mean that all Indian food is extremely hot and spicy, as many people believe. The dishes can be as hot or as mild as the individual family chooses, since this is a matter of personal taste. The best Indian dishes are a clever blend of exotic spices, delicate herbs with vegetables or meat.

Indian curries are delicious and can be prepared with just a few simple ingredients. The secret of producing these aromatic delicacies is adding the right ingredient at the right time, thus following the correct sequence of cooking. In many recipes of curries, nonfat plain yogurt has been used instead of cream, for healthy eating. Low fat milk is added in addition to water to prepare wet curries, imparting a lovely texture, taste and colour to the gravies.

Pulses and lentils (*Dals*) form an important part of an Indian meal. Aromatic cumin seeds dropped in hot oil and cooked on low heat till golden, added to pulses, change them completely. On the other hand, if the cumin seeds get burnt, a mess is produced. The book explains very clearly, how to flavour your pulses the right way!

The vegetables and meat are eaten with rice or Indian breads (*roti*). Exotic *biryaanis* and *pulaos* prepared from Indian *basmati* rice, flavoured with magical spices like fennel seeds, cinnamon sticks and cardamom pods, are all explained simply. The Indian flat breads - *nans*, *phulkas* and *paranthas* are just wonderful! The book tells you how just a few black sesame seeds and shredded almonds add that special touch to the simple *nans*, making them exotic!

I have tried to make the recipes as simple as possible, giving step-by-step instructions, allowing you to enjoy the exotic flavour and aroma of Indian food, any time of the week.

Nita Mehta

ABOUT THE RECIPES
WHAT'S IN A CUP?
INDIAN CUP
1 teacup = 200 ml liquid
AMERICAN CUP
1 cup = 240 ml liquid (8 oz)
The recipes in this book were tested with the Indian teacup which holds 200 ml liquid.

Contents

Drinks & Shorbas 16

Snacks   21

Curries   37

Herbs & Spices

ENGLISH NAME	HINDI NAME
1. Asafoetida	1. Hing
2. Bay Leaves	2. Tej Patta
3. Cardamom	3. Elaichi, Chhoti Elaichi
4. Cardamom, Black	4. Moti Elaichi
5. Carom Seeds	5. Ajwain
6. Chillies, Green	6. Hari Mirch
7. Chillies, Dry Red	7. Sukhi Sabut Lal Mirch
8. Chilli Powder, Red	8. Lal Mirch Powder
9. Cinnamon	9. Dalchini
10. Cloves	10. Laung
11. Coriander Seeds	11. Sabut Dhania
12. Coriander Seeds, ground	12. Dhania Powder
13. Coriander Leaves	13. Hara Dhania
14. Cumin Seeds	14. Jeera
15. Cumin Seeds, black	15. Shah Jeera
16. Curry Leaves	16. Kari Patta
17. Fennel Seeds	17. Saunf
18. Fenugreek Seeds	18. Methi Dana
19. Fenugreek Leaves, Dried	19. Kasuri Methi
20. Garam Masala Powder	20. Garam Masala (see p. 8)
21. Garlic	21. Lahsun
22. Ginger	22. Adrak
23. Mace	23. Javitri
24. Mango Powder, Dried	24. Amchur
25. Melon Seeds	25. Magaz
26. Mint Leaves	26. Pudina
27. Mustard Seeds	27. Rai, Sarson
28. Nigella, Onion Seeds	28. Kalaunji
29. Nutmeg	29. Jaiphal
30. Peppercorns	30. Sabut Kali Mirch
31. Pomegranate Seeds, Dried	31. Anardana
32. Sesame Seeds	32. Til
33. Saffron	33. Kesar
34. Turmeric Powder	34. Haldi

Home made Indian Spice Blends

To perk up the flavour of Indian dishes.

GARAM MASALA

Makes ¼ cup

5-6 2" sticks cinnamon (*dalchini*)
15-20 black cardamom pods (*moti elaichi*)
¾ tbsp cloves (*laung*)
2 tbsp black peppercorns (*saboot kali mirch*)
2 tbsp cumin seeds (*jeera*)
½ flower of mace (*javitri*)

1. Remove seeds of black cardamoms. Discard skin.
2. Roast all ingredients together in a skillet for 2 minutes on low heat, stirring constantly, till fragrant.
3. Remove from heat. Cool. Grind to a fine powder in a clean coffee or spice grinder. Store in a small jar with a tight. fitting lid.

CHAAT MASALA

Makes ¾ cup

3 tbsp cumin seeds (*jeera*)
1 tbsp ground ginger (*sonth*)
2 tsp carom seeds (*ajwain*)
2 tsp raw mango powder (*amchoor*)
2 tbsp ground black salt (*kala namak*)
1 tsp salt, 1 tsp ground black pepper
½ tsp ground nutmeg (*jaiphal*)

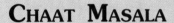

1. Roast cumin seeds in a small nonstick skillet or a wok to a golden brown colour. Transfer to a bowl and set aside.
2. Roast carom seeds over moderate heat for about 2 minutes, till fragrant.
3. Grind roasted cumin seeds and carom seeds. Mix in the remaining ingredients.
4. Store in an air-tight jar.

TANDOORI MASALA

Makes ½ cup

2 tbsp coriander seeds (*saboot dhania*)
2 tbsp cumin seeds (*jeera*)
1 tsp fenugreek seeds (*methi daana*)
1 tbsp black peppercorns (*saboot kali mirch*)
1 tbsp cloves (*laung*)
seeds of 8 black cardamom pods (*moti elaichi*)
2 tsp paprika (*degi mirch*)
1 tbsp dried fenugreek leaves (*kasoori methi*)
1 tbsp ground cinnamon (*dalchini*)
½ tbsp ground ginger (*sonth*)
½ tsp red chilli powder

1. In a nonstick skillet, roast together — coriander seeds, cumin seeds, fenugreek seeds, black peppercorns, cloves and cardamom seeds, on moderate heat for about 1 minute, until fragrant.
2. Remove from heat and let the spices cool down. Grind to a fine powder. Transfer to a bowl and mix in the remaining ingredients. Store in an air tight jar.

SAMBHAR POWDER

Makes ½ cup

¼ cup coriander seeds *(saboot dhania)*
1 tbsp cumin seeds *(jeera)*
1 tbsp dried, split yellow chick peas *(channe ki dal)*
2 tsp fenugreek seeds *(methi daana)*
5-6 dry, red chillies *(saboot lal mirch)*
½ tsp asafoetida *(hing)*
1½ tsp peppercorns *(saboot kali mirch)*

1. Roast all ingredients together over low heat in a nonstick skillet, until fragrant.
2. Cool the spices and grind to a fine powder in a small coffee grinder. Store in an air tight jar.

The Indian Spice Box

Almost every Indian kitchen has this box with various compartments to hold the basic spices & salt.

Dhania Powder

Salt

Amchoor

Garam Masala

Jeera

Haldi

Red Chilli Powder

Some Cooking Utensils

KADHAI (wok) - The kadhai is a deep pan, round bottomed with two handles on the sides. Used mainly for frying and making Indian masala dishes. When buying one, choose a heavy-bottomed one in a medium size. Steel/Brass kadhais were used earlier, but now aluminium or non-stick ones are more popular. Copper-bottomed metal kadhais are also becoming popular.

TAWA (griddle) - A heavy iron tawa makes good chappatis. Buy one with a handle. These days non stick griddles are also available.

Sauce Pan - These are deep pans with a handle. Useful for making tea, blanching vegetables in water or working with food where some sauce is needed. Usually these are made of stainless steel and are available in various sizes. Nonstick ones are also available.

PATILA (deep metal pans) - Used for boiling water, milk, rice, pasta etc. Buy a heavy-bottom one. Deep non-stick pots with handles are also available which are very handy for making soups, rice and curries.

Non Stick Frying Pan (saute pan, skillet)

- A pan about 2" high is ideal for shallow frying tikkis, kebabs and other snacks. It makes a good utensil for cooking dry/semi dry dishes too. The vegetables lie flat in a single layer on the wide bottom making them crunchy on the outside and yet moist from inside. Remember to use a plastic or a wooden spoon/spatula to stir and fry in all nonstick vessels. Metallic ones will scratch the non stick finish and ruin it. Avoid strong detergents for washing them, warm soapy water is best. It is good to have one small (about 7" diameter) and one big (10 " diameter) pan. Dosas and pancakes too can be made conveniently in them.

Kadcchi (laddle) - Large, long

- handled spoon with a small shallow bowl like spoon at the end. Should be strong enough for stirring masalas.

Palta (pancake turner) - These

broad metal turners have thin, flexible yet sturdy blade that will slide easily under the food and then be strong enough to turn the food. Not just for pancakes, it's great for turning kebabs too. Ideally choose one with a heat-resistant handle.

Chakla-Belan (rolling board-rolling pin)

- A marble or heavy weight rolling board is ideal for rolling out dough for chapatis, poori etc. A wooden rolling pin with it makes the set complete. Plastic rolling pins are available but I am not too comfortable with them.

Parat (shallow bowl to knead dough)

- Shallow bowl to make dough, generally stainless steel. Buy a medium size even if you are a small family, because if the bowl is too small, the surrounding area tends to get messy while making the dough. Dough can also be made in a food processor.

Chhanni (large steel colander)

A big, wide strainer with large holes for draining cooked rice, pasta and for draining fresh vegetables after washing.

Chhara, Pauni (slotted spoon)

- A big round, flat spoon with holes and a long handle. Good for removing fried food from oil as it drains out the oil nicely through the holes. Also used to lift solid foods out of cooking liquids.

Tips on Tandoori, Dals, Breads & Rice

Tips which you must go through for perfect results.....

Tips for Tandoori & Other Snacks

- An oily snack is not appetizing, so make it a habit to transfer the fried snack from oil on to a tissue or a *paper napkin* to absorb the excess oil.

- A few crisp leaves of lettuce or a sprig of mint or coriander placed at the edge of the serving platter makes the snack irresistible! Make the green leaves crisp by putting them in a bowl of cold water and keeping them in the fridge for 3-4 hours or even overnight. Some cucumber slices or tomato wedges placed along with the greens, beautify it further.

- For getting a crisp coating on cutlets or rolls, dip prepared snack in a thin batter of maida and water and then roll in bread crumbs. Fry till well browned.

- A teaspoon of til (sesame seeds) or khus-khus (poppy seeds) or ajwain (carom seeds), added to coating mixture or bread crumbs makes the snack interesting.

- In the absence of bread crumbs, a mixture of ¼ cup maida and ½ cup suji may be used to get a crisp coating.

- If your cutlets fall apart, quickly tear 1-2 slices of bread and grind in a mixer to get fresh bread crumbs. Add it to the cutlet mixture for binding.

- To make crisp potato chips, soak sliced potatoes in cold water for 1 hour. Drain. Wipe dry and sprinkle some maida (plain flour) on them before frying.

- Never start frying in smoking hot oil as it will turn the snack black. Never fry in cold oil as the snack may fall apart or it may soak a lot of oil.

- For deep frying any snack, add small quantities to the oil at one time. This maintains the oil's temperature. If too many pieces are added together, the oil turns cold and a lot of oil is then absorbed by the snack.

- After deep frying, let the oil cool down. Add a little quantity of fresh oil to the used oil before reusing. This prevents the oil from discolouring.

Tips for Cooking Dal

- Soak whole pulses (saboot dals) overnight or soak in boiling water for 20 minutes, to soften skin. Use the same water for cooking in which pulses have been soaked.
- Add a few drops of oil or ghee during cooking to reduce cooking time and frothing.
- Do not use cooking soda as it destroys the vitamin B content.
- If 1 cup dal is to be cooked, add 3-4 cups water to it, depending on the type of dal. Well cooked & blended dals taste better.

Tips for Making Rotis/Breads

- Knead dough well and keep it covered for half an hour before using, to allow gluten strands to develop. If this is not done, its puffing quality is affected and the edges become cracked.
- Use appropriate amount of water to make the dough so that it does not become too dry or too wet in cooking. Cereals have different hydration capacity. For example, atta needs about 60 percent water (by weight) to form a soft dough for chapatis and paranthas.
- Add less water for making a firm dough for pooris and kachoris.
- Do not use too much dry flour in rolling the dough.
- Use a heavy griddle for cooking chapatis and paranthas.
- Heat ghee to smoking point before frying pooris. Later reduce flame.

Tips for Boiling Rice

- Always use good quality rice. The older the rice, the better the cooking quality.
- Wash and drain rice repeatedly until the runoff water is clear. Keep the rice soaked in fresh water for half an hour.
- For 1 cup of rice, put 5 - 6 cups of water to boil in a large pan . Add the rice, after the water boils. For steaming rice, use double the quantity of water. 1 cup rice will need 2 cups water for steamed rice.
- 1-2 tsp lemon juice may be added to whiten & separate the rice grains.
- When boiling rice in excess water, drain away the water as soon as the rice is just cooked. Avoid overcooking, which produces a mash. Cool in a broad vessel.
- Do not cover it. Fluff it with a fork to let the steam escape, so that the grains do not stick to each other.
- 1 cup uncooked rice will give about 2-2½ cups boiled rice.

drinks & shorbas

Drinks & Shorbas

Gajar ki Kanji

Celebrate Holi or any special occasion with this attractive drink – cold, sharp and spicy!

Serves 8

500 gm black carrots (*kali gajar*)
3 tsp salt
1 tsp black salt (*kala namak*)
¼ tsp asafoetida (*hing*)
2 tsp coarsely ground dry red chillies
3 tbsp ground yellow mustard seeds (*rai*) powder
8-10 cups water

1. Peel, wash and cut the carrots into thin long fingers.
2. Mix carrots with all the other ingredients in a bowl.
3. Put in a glass jar, seal well and leave for 4-5 days to ferment at room temperature.
4. Put in the refrigerator till serving time. Serve chilled.

Note: If black carrots are not available then substitute them with regular carrots and a small beetroot.

The maturing of any kanji will depend upon the temperature; if the weather is warm the kanji will be ready earlier. Therefore keep checking every day.

Southern Tomato Rasam

This traditional thin tomato soup is a hot and spicy appetizer to awaken your taste buds.

Serves 6-8

1 kg tomatoes - each cut into 4 pieces
3 cups water
1 tbsp oil
2-3 whole, dry red chillies or ½ tsp paprika
1 tsp cumin seeds (*jeera*)
1 tsp mustard seeds (*rai*)
¼ tsp asafoetida (*hing*)
a few curry leaves (*curry patta*)
¼ tsp ground turmeric (*haldi*)
1½ tsp salt, or to taste
1½ tsp peppercorns (*saboot kali mirch*)
8- 10 flakes of garlic

1. Crush the flakes of garlic roughly without peeling the flakes. Separately, crush or pound the peppercorns too.

2. Boil tomatoes with 3 cups water. Keep on low heat for about 10 minutes, till tomatoes turn soft. Remove from heat and cool. Blend to a puree.

3. Heat 1 tbsp oil. Reduce heat and fry the red chillies till they turn a shade darker. Add together - cumin seeds, mustard seeds and asafoetida. When cumin turns golden, add curry leaves.

4. Add the pureed tomatoes, salt and haldi.

5. Add the crushed garlic and peppercorns to the tomatoes. Boil. Simmer for 10 minutes. Remove from heat.

6. Strain. Discard the ingredients in the strainer. Serve rasam garnished with coriander leaves.

Kashmiri Kehwa

A saffron-scented special tea from Kashmir enriched with almonds.

Makes 2 cups

2¼ cups water
1 tsp green tea leaves
2 tsp sugar, or to taste
2 green cardamoms (*chhoti elaichi*) -
powdered
2 pinches of cinnamon (*dalchini*) powder
4-6 strands of saffron (*kesar*)

TOPPING
3-4 almonds (*badaam*) - slivered
(cut into thin long pieces)

1. Mix all the ingredients in a saucepan. Boil. Simmer for 5 minutes.
2. Strain tea into the cups.
3. Top each cup with some slivered almonds. Serve hot.

Note: Kehwa is good for digestion. You can omit sugar if desired.

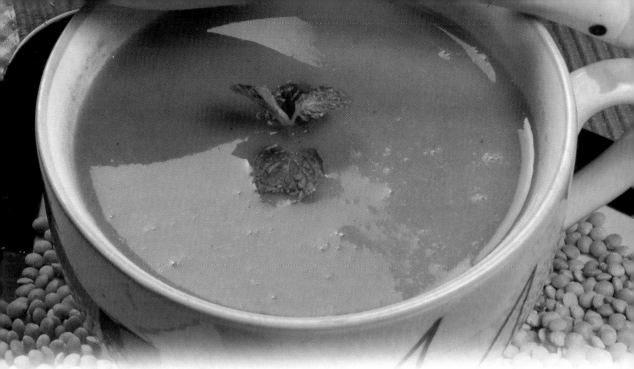

Mutton Mulligatawny

Bring back the days of the Raj to your table with this coconut-flavoured hearty soup.

Serves 4-5

350-400 gm lamb (*mutton*)
(boneless) - cut into ¼" pieces
1 tbsp butter
½ cup chopped onions
1 tsp minced garlic, a few curry leaves
½ cup orange lentils (*dhuli masoor dal*)
½ cup chopped apple
1 cup ready-made coconut milk
2 tsp curry powder
½-¾ tsp paprika, salt, pepper to taste
2 tbsp boiled rice
1 tbsp lemon juice

1. Melt butter in a deep pan. Add onions, garlic and curry leaves. Saute for a minute.

2. Add mutton, lentils and apple. Stir for 5 minutes on medium heat.

3. Add curry powder and paprika. Stir. Add 6 cups water. Bring to a boil. Simmer for 30 minutes. Strain. Pick up the mutton pieces. Grind the residue in the strainer in a mixer with a little liquid. Strain it back into the soup.

4. Cut the mutton into tiny pieces. Add 1 cup coconut milk and mutton pieces to the soup. Add salt and pepper. Bring to a boil. Check the seasoning and add more salt and pepper if required. Add lemon juice to taste.

5. Serve hot in soup bowls, sprinkled with a tsp of boiled rice, garnished with mint.

snacks

Snacks

Moong Dal Tilli Pakore

*In this speciality from Delhi, paneer cubes, tomatoes and capsicums are skewered on toothpicks (*tilli*), and dipped in a thick batter made from moong dal to give a crusty coating when deep-fried – no wonder they are so famous!*

Makes 24 pieces

200 gm paneer - cut into ¾" squares of ¼-½" thickness
1 large capsicum - cut into ¾" pieces
2 tomatoes - cut into 4 pieces lengthwise, pulp removed and cut into ¾" pieces
some chaat masala
24 toothpicks

BATTER
½ cup dehusked moog beans (*dhuli moong dal*) - soaked for 1-2 hours
2 tbsp cornflour
2 tbsp fresh coriander - chopped very finely
1 green chilli - chopped very finely
½ tsp salt, or to taste
½ tsp red chilli powder
1 tsp coriander (*dhania*) powder
¼ tsp dried mango powder (*amchoor*)
½ tsp garam masala
1-2 pinches of tandoori red colour (optional)

1. Soak dal for 1-2 hours. Strain. Grind in a mixer with little water to a smooth thick paste. Put in a bowl. Beat well by hand to make it light.

2. Add cornflour, coriander, green chilli, salt, red chilli powder, dhania powder, amchoor and garam masala to dal paste. Add colour. Add a little water to get a coating consistency. Keep aside.

3. Thread a capsicum, then a paneer and then a tomato piece on each tooth pick. Keep them spaced out on the stick. Keep aside till serving time.

4. To serve, heat oil for deep frying. Dip the paneer sticks in the prepared dal batter. Shake off the excess batter.

5. Deep fry 6-8 sticks at a time till golden. Serve hot sprinkled generously with chat masala.

Seekh Lahori

Recapture the taste of a night in the crowded bazaars of old Lahore with this authentic but easy recipe.

Serves 6

800 gm mutton mince (*keema*)
1 onion - finely chopped
1½" piece of ginger - finely chopped
8 flakes of garlic - finely chopped
4 green chillies - deseeded & finely chopped
3 tbsp chopped coriander
2 eggs
4 tbsp grated cheddar cheese
½ tsp chopped mint (*poodina*)
2 tbsp roasted gram flour (*besan*)

LAHORI SEEKH MASALA
1 tsp pomegranate seeds (*anaar daana*)
1 tsp black peppercorns (*saboot kali mirch*)
seeds of 2 green cardamom (*chhoti elaichi*)
seeds of 1 black cardamom (*moti elaichi*)
1" stick cinnamon stick (*dalchini*)
2 clove (*laung*)
a pinch of nutmeg (*jaiphal*)
¾ tsp rock salt (*kala namak*)

BASTING
desi ghee or melted butter for basting

1. Wash the mince (keema) in a strainer and gently press to squeeze out all the water. Grind in a grinder to make it fine.
2. Powder all ingredients for lahori seekh masala together in a small grinder.
3. In a bowl add mince, onion, ginger, garlic, green chillies, coriander, eggs, cheese, mint, besan & the ground spices, mix well. Divide into 16-18 balls and keep aside for 2 hours.
4. Heat an oven with greased skewers at 180°C. Cover the wire rack of the oven with foil. Grease the foil well with oil.
5. Take one ball of the mince mixture at a time and hold a hot skewer carefully in the other hand. Carefully press the mince on to the hot skewer. The mince will immediately stick to the skewer.
6. Make another seekh on the same skewer, leaving a gap of 2". Repeat with the left over mince on all the other skewers.
7. Place the skewers on the wire rack with foil. Put in the oven. Cook for 10-15 minutes, change sides, baste with ghee or melted butter. Cook for another 5 minutes. When cooked, gently remove the kebab from the skewers with the help of a cloth. Serve cut into 2" pieces with mint chutney.

Delhi ke Fruit Kulle

Hollowed cups of charcoal-roasted potatoes are sold on the streets of Old Delhi. However, the potatoes can be boiled for a more practical version for the home kitchen. It started with potatoes and now kullas of all kinds of fruits and vegetables have become popular.

Serves 6

3 small potatoes - boiled
3 small tomatoes
1 cucumber (*kheera*) - cut into 1½" long pieces

FILLING
½ cup channas (*safeed chhole*) - soak in warm water for 1 hour
½ cup fresh pomegranate kernels (*anaar ke daane*)
½ cup grapes (use black or green) - each cut into half from the middle
½ cup peas (*matar*) - boiled
2-3 green chillies - deseeded and chopped
1-2 tbsp chaat masala, preferably kala chaat masala
½ tsp roasted cumin (*bhuna jeera*) powder
juice of ½ lemon, salt to taste

1. Drain channas. Put them in a pressure cooker with 1 tsp salt and 1 cup water. Pressure cook to give 1 whistle. Remove from fire. Strain channas after pressure drops. Leave them in strainer (channi) for all the water to drain out.

2. Peel the boiled potatoes. Cut each potato into 2 halves. Scoop out each piece with the help of a scooper or knife to get hollow cups. Sprinkle some lemon juice and chat masala in the potato cups and rub well. Keep aside.

3. Cut the tomato into halves and scoop out the filling. Similarly scoop out the cucumber pieces with a knife or scooper, keeping the base intact. Sprinkle some lemon juice and chat masala in the cups.

4. For filling, mix all ingredients in a bowl. Check the filling and make it to your taste. Keep aside.

5. Fill each hollowed vegetable with this filling, heaping it a little. Serve.

Amritsari Fish

The beauty of these golden, batter-fried fingers is that the delicate taste and texture of fish (preferably sole) is not overwhelmed with spices – just one shining accent note of ajwain (carom seeds).

Serves 5-6

500 gm boneless fish fillet - cut into
1½" long pieces, 10- 12 pieces)
¼ tsp turmeric powder (*haldi*)
1 tsp salt
1 tbsp lemon juice
2 tbsp gram flour (*besan*)

BATTER
3 tbsp flour (*maida*)
4 tbsp cornflour
3 tbsp gram flour (*besan*)
1 egg
1 tsp carom seeds (*ajwain*)
2 tsp garlic paste
2 tsp ginger paste
¾ tsp salt
1½ tsp red chilli powder
1 tbsp lemon juice
a pinch of colour
¼ cup water, approx.

TO SERVE
some chaat masala for sprinkling on top
hari chutney
one large lemon - cut into wedges

1. Cut fish into 1½" long pieces of ¼" thickness.
2. Rub fish pieces with haldi, salt, lemon juice and besan. Keep aside for 20 minutes. Wash well to remove all smell. Pat dry on a clean kitchen towel.
3. Mix together all ingredients of the batter to get a pouring batter of thin coating consistency.
4. Leave the fish to marinate in it for at least 2 hours or till serving time in the fridge.
5. At the time of serving, heat oil on medium heat. Pick up the fish pieces, deep fry to a golden colour on low medium heat till the fish is cooked and crisp.
6. Sprinkle chaat masala and serve hot garnished with lemon wedges and sprigs of coriander or mint.

Note: For a different flavour 1-1½ tsp dry fenugreek leaves (*kasoori methi*) can be added to the batter.

Jhinga Til Tinka

A sensuous experience! Bite into a sesame-flavoured crumbly coating; then go to deeper layers of textured and creamy secrets, scented with subtle spices.

Makes 16

500 gm medium sized prawns - cleaned and deveined
juice of ½ lemon
oil for deep fry

1ST MARINADE
5 tsp garlic paste (16-18 flakes of garlic)
4 tsp ginger paste (2" piece of ginger)
½ tsp white or black pepper powder
½ tsp red chilli powder
¼ tsp salt
4 tbsp lemon juice

2ND MARINADE
½ cup yogurt (*dahi*)
½ tsp salt
a pinch of tandoori colour
½ cup grated cheddar cheese
1½ tsp carom seeds (*ajwain*)
¼ cup cream
½ tsp green cardamom (*chhoti elaichi*) powder
3 tbsp gram flour (*besan*)

COATING
2 tbsp black sesame seeds (*til*)
1 cup fresh bread-crumbs (grind 2 bread slices in a blender to get fresh crumbs)

1. Sprinkle ½ tsp salt and juice of ½ lemon. Mix and keep aside for 15 minutes. Wash well and pat dry.
2. Mix all the ingredients of the 1st marinade in a bowl. Add prawns and mix gently. Keep aside for 30 minutes.
3. Mix all ingredients of the 2nd marinade in another bowl. Mix well. Add prawns with the 1st marinade to the 2nd marinade in the bowl. Keep aside for 30 minutes.
4. Skewer one prawn on each wooden stick or big toothpicks.
5. Mix bread-crumbs with sesame seeds, roll the skewered prawns in the coating mixture and refrigerate for 15 minutes.
6. Heat oil in a kadhai and deep fry 1-2 pieces at a time over medium heat for 2-3 minutes. Serve with poodina chutney.

Tandoori Bharwaan Aloo

What a combination! Scooped potatoes filled with paneer, almonds and thick yogurt - then baked in a tandoor.

Serves 3-4

3 big (longish) potatoes
some chaat masala to sprinkle

FILLING

3 almonds (*badaam*) - crushed roughly with a rolling pin (*belan*)
1 tbsp mint (*poodina*) leaves - chopped
1 green chilli - slit, remove seeds & chop
4 tbsp grated paneer (50 gm)
¼ tsp salt or to taste, ¼ tsp garam masala
¼ tsp red chilli powder
a pinch dried mango powder (*amchoor*)

COVERING

½ cup thick curd - hang in a muslin cloth for 30 minutes, 1 tbsp ginger paste
¼ tsp red chilli powder, ¾ tsp salt
¼ tsp red or orange tandoori colour or turmeric (*haldi*)

BHARWAAN ALOO MASALA

1 tsp black cumin (*shah jeera*)
seeds of 2 brown cardamom (*moti elaichi*)
6-8 peppercorns (*saboot kali mirch*)
2-3 blades of mace (*javetri*)

1. Boil potatoes in salted water till just tender. Do not over boil. When they are no longer hot, peel skin.
2. For the filling, mix crushed almonds with mint leaves, green chillies, grated paneer, salt, garam masala, red chilli and amchoor.
3. Grind or crush shah jeera, seeds of moti elaichi, peppercorns and 2-3 pinches of javetri to a coarse powder.
4. To the paneer filling, add ¼-½ teaspoon of the above freshly ground masala powder also. Keep the leftover powder aside.
5. For the covering, mix hung curd, ginger paste, remaining freshly ground masala powder, red chilli and salt. Add haldi or orange colour.
6. Run the tip of a fork on the back surface of the potatoes, making the surface rough. (The rough surface holds the curd well). Cut each potato into 2 halves, vertically. Scoop out, just a little, to get a small cavity in each potato with the back of a teaspoon. Stuff with paneer filling.
7. With a spoon apply the curd on the back and sides of the potato.
8. Grill potatoes in a gas tandoor or a preheated oven for 15 minutes on a greased wire rack till they get slightly dry.
9. Spoon some oil or melted butter on them (baste) and then grill further till the coating turns absolutely dry. Sprinkle some chaat masala and serve hot.

33

Mughlai Malai Tikka

Soak chicken cubes in a classic cream marinade – grill while basting with butter to make moist mouth-watering morsels. Be sure to make a large quantity to serve as appetizers to young men who have their drinks in hand!

Serves 6-7

500 gm boneless chicken - cut into 1½" pieces

MARINADE
¾ cup thick cream
¼ tsp green cardamom powder (seeds of 2-3 *chhoti elaichi* - crushed)
1 tsp white or black pepper powder
1 tsp garlic paste
2 tsp ginger paste
3 tbsp cornflour
1 tbsp melted butter or ghee
½ tsp garam masala powder
¼ tsp dried mango powder (*amchoor*)
½ tsp cumin seeds (*jeera*) powder
1½ tsp salt
1 green chilli - crushed, optional

BASTING
2 tbsp melted butter or oil

1. Mix all the ingredients of the marinade- cream, chhoti elaichi powder, white pepper, ginger-garlic paste, cornflour, melted butter, garam masala, amchoor, jeera powder, salt and green chillies.
2. Marinate chicken covered with a plastic wrap/cling film for 2 hours or till serving time in the refrigerator.
3. Heat an oven at 180°C or heat a gas tandoor on gas for 15 minutes on low heat. Cover the wire rack with aluminium foil. Grease foil with oil.
4. Place the well coated chicken pieces on the greased grill or skewer the chicken pieces. Roast for 10 minutes or until cooked, thoroughly basting (brushing) with melted butter or oil at least once in between. Roast for another 5 minutes.
5. Sprinkle chaat masala and serve hot with poodina chutney.

Note:

- Grilling or roasting should be done on constant moderate heat, otherwise it toughens the protein of the meat, making the kebabs shrink and turn hard. Always grease the wire rack or grill nicely with oil to avoid the kebabs sticking to the grill.

- Cover the tray beneath the wire rack or the skewers with aluminium foil to collect the drippings of the tikkas.

Dahi Kebab

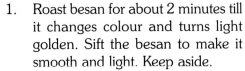

Hung yogurt is thickened with roasted gram flour (besan) and shaped into incredibly light kebabs – these are carefully coated with golden fried onions dissolved in milk!

Makes 8-10

2 cups yogurt - hang in a muslin cloth for 3-4 hours to drain off liquid completely
½ cup gram flour (*besan*)
2 tsp garlic paste
¾ cup oil to shallow fry
1 onion - cut into slices
¼ cup milk to sprinkle

DAHI KEBAB MASALA
seeds of 4 green cardamoms (*chhoti elaichi*)
½" stick cinnamon (*dalchini*)
8-10 cloves (*laung*)
½ tsp black pepper, 1 tsp salt
1½-2 tsp red chilli powder

1. Roast besan for about 2 minutes till it changes colour and turns light golden. Sift the besan to make it smooth and light. Keep aside.
2. Heat oil in a frying pan. Fry sliced onions till golden brown, remove and grind to a paste. Keep fried onion paste aside till serving time.
3. Crush elaichi, dalchini and laung for dahi kebab masala. Add salt, pepper and red chilli to it. Keep masala powder aside.
4. Mix 2 tsp of the above masala powder to the hung yogurt, keeping the remaining masala powder for use in step 6. Add garlic and besan also and mix well. Divide into 20 equal parts. Flatten, wetting hands with a little water to give the kebabs smooth and even shape. Chill in the fridge for atleast 30 min.
5. Heat the oil in the pan and fry the kebabs on low heat, turning after a minute to brown both sides. Keep aside till serving time.
6. To serve, put fried onion paste in the pan on low heat. Add the remaining masala powder, stir and add the fried kebabs. Gently mix. Sprinkle milk on the kebabs, turn side and sprinkle milk on the other side too. Remove and serve at once.

CURRIES

Curries

Dum ki Arbi

Arbi gets a gourmet image in this amazing curry, made with yogurt and boiled onion paste, thickened with poppy seeds and cooked slowly and lovingly.

Serves 4

400 gm colocasia (*arbi*)
2 tbsp poppy seeds (*khus khus*)
3 onions
1" piece of ginger
12 flakes of garlic
1 tsp coriander (*dhania*) powder
½ tsp red chilli powder
1 tsp cumin (*jeera*)
½ tsp garam masala powder
1 tsp salt or to taste
½ tsp turmeric powder (*haldi*)
4- 6 green cardamom (*chhoti elaichi*)
2 cups yogurt (*dahi*)
a pinch of nutmeg (*jaiphal*) - grated
oil to deep fry
coriander leaves to garnish

1. Soak khus-khus in ¼ cup water. Keep aside.
2. Peel and cut arbi into 1" pieces. Deep fry in hot oil till golden brown.
3. Peel onions and cut into 4 pieces and put in a saucepan with 2 cups of water. Boil onions for 3-4 minutes till soft. Drain. Cool.
4. Grind the onion, soaked poppy seeds, ginger, garlic, coriander powder, red chilli powder, cumin, garam masala, salt and turmeric powder in a blender to a paste.
5. Heat 2 tbsp oil in a pan. Add green cardamoms, stir for a minute.
6. Add prepared paste. Saute till light golden brown.
7. Mix yogurt with ½ cup water. Add the yogurt stirring continuously; bring it to a boil.
8. Add arbi and grated nutmeg.
9. Cover the pan with a tightfitting lid and simmer for 15 minutes. Alternatively cover the pan with aluminium foil or seal the lid with wheat flour dough, so that the aroma is contained in the pan and does not escape.
10. Garnish with coriander and serve.

Lucknawi Koftas

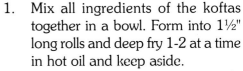

*These potato and spinach koftas are simmered in delicate gravy enriched with almonds,
melon seeds and poppy seeds – a marvel of tastes and aromas.*

Serves 4

KOFTAS
125 gm potatoes - boiled and mashed
¼ cup chopped coriander
¼ cup cornflour
½ cup chopped spinach (*palak*)
2 tbsp dry fenugreek leaves (*kasoori methi*)
½ tsp garam masala
1 tbsp lemon juice
1 tsp salt, or to taste
oil for deep frying

MASALA PASTE
12 almonds (*badaam*)
4 tbsp melon seeds (*magaz*)
6 green chillies
4 tbsp poppy seeds (*khus khus*)
1 onion
½" piece of ginger
3-4 flakes of garlic

OTHER INGREDIENTS
3 tbsp oil
2 onions - finely chopped
1 cup yogurt (*dahi*)
½ cup milk
¼ cup cream
½ tsp turmeric (*haldi*)
½ cup water
1 tsp sugar
1 tsp salt

1. Mix all ingredients of the koftas together in a bowl. Form into 1½" long rolls and deep fry 1-2 at a time in hot oil and keep aside.

2. Grind all ingredients for the masala paste together in a mixer to a fine paste.

3. For the gravy, heat 3 tbsp oil add chopped onions, stir till golden brown.

4. Add the ground masala paste and fry for a 2- 3 minutes.

5. Reduce heat, stirring continuously add yogurt, milk, cream, turmeric, sugar and salt. Increase heat bring to a boil, stirring continuously.

6. Add ½ cup water and cook for another 5 minutes. Remove from fire and keep aside till serving time.

7. At the time of serving heat up the gravy add the koftas and simmer for a minute for the koftas to get hot. Serve hot.

Goan Fish Curry

Another landscape, another cuisine – this curry has tamarind and coconut milk, curry leaves and black mustard seeds.

Serves 4

400 gm of any firm white fish - cut into 2" pieces
4 tbsp oil
2-3 green chillies - deseeded and sliced
1 tsp red chilli powder
2 tsp coriander (*dhania*) powder
½ tsp garam masala
1 tsp salt
2 cups thick coconut milk
2 tbsp tamarind (*imli*) pulp, optional
1 cup water

PASTE
1 medium onion
2½" piece of ginger
8-10 flakes of garlic

TEMPERING (*TADKA*)
2 tbsp oil
1 tsp black mustard seeds (*sarson seeds*)
8-10 curry leaves (*curry patta*)
3 whole dry red chillies

1. Make a paste of the onion, ginger and garlic in a blender.
2. Heat the oil in a kadhai, add onion paste from blender and green chillies. Cook until onion turns brown.
3. Add red chilli powder, dhania powder, garam masala and salt. Mix. Cook on medium heat until oil separates. Sprinkle a little water if the masala sticks to the pan.
4. Add imli pulp, coconut milk and 1 cup of water. Let it come to a boil. Add fish and cook on low heat for 10-12 minutes or until the fish is cooked. Remove from fire.
5. For the tempering, heat the oil in a frying pan add all the ingredients. When the seeds start spluttering pour over the hot fish. Serve hot.

Rajasthani Gatte ki Subzi

A dough made of gram flour is used to make the steamed gatte. *The curry has a base of curd, gram flour and pureed tomatoes – spicy, chilli hot and brightly coloured like the place of its origin.*

Serves 4-5

GATTE
¾ cup gram flour (*besan*)
¼ tsp baking soda (*mitha soda*)
½ tsp ginger-green chilli paste
¼ tsp carom seeds (*ajwain*)
¼ tsp fennel (*saunf*) - crushed
½ tsp salt
½ tsp turmeric (*haldi*)
½ tsp red chilli powder
½ tsp coriander (*dhania*) powder
½ tsp garam masala
2 tbsp yogurt (*dahi*)
1 tbsp oil

CURRY
2 tbsp oil
2 cloves (*laung*)
1 tsp cumin seeds (*jeera*)
1 cardamom (*moti elaichi*) - crushed
¼ tsp turmeric (*haldi*)
½ tsp red chilli powder
2 tomatoes - puree in a mixer & strain
½ tsp ginger paste
1 green chilli - crushed
1 cup yogurt mixed with 2 tsp gram flour
(*besan*) & 1 cup water till smooth

1. Sift besan and soda. Add ginger chilli paste, ajwain, saunf, powdered spices and just enough curd to get a very soft dough. Mix well. Mix 1 tbsp oil and knead again. Make 4 balls.
   With the help of oil smeared on your hands, roll out thin fingers 3"-4" long, like cylinders.

2. Boil 5 cups of water. Keep the gatte in a stainless steel round strainer and keep the strainer on the pan of boiling water and cover with a lid.

3. Steam gatte for 5-7 minutes. Let them cool. Later cut them into rounds of ½" thickness. Keep aside.

4. For curry, blend curd, besan and 1 cup water in a mixer till very smooth. Puree tomatoes and strain them to get a smooth puree.

5. Heat 2 tbsp oil, add laung, jeera, moti elaichi, haldi and red chilli powder. Stir.

6. Add tomato puree, ginger and crushed chilli. Cook for 3 minutes till dry and oil separates.

7. Reduce heat. Add curd with besan. Stir constantly, on low heat to bring it to a boil. Simmer for 3-4 minutes.

8. Add gatte. Cook for 2-3 minutes. Serve hot garnished with hara dhania.

Goan Chicken Xacuti

The word xacuti is pronounced 'shakuti'. An all-time favourite of Goan food lovers, it is a sell-out in most Goan restaurants. Learn to make it at home with these clear instructions.

Serves 6

800 gm chicken - cut into 12 pieces
4 tbsp oil
2 medium sized onions - finely chopped
salt to taste
2 cups water
1 tbsp tamarind (*imli*) pulp
¼ tsp nutmeg (*jaiphal*) - grated

DRY ROASTED MASALA PASTE
4-6 flakes of garlic
1 cup grated fresh coconut
2" stick of cinnamon (*dalchini*)
6 cloves (*laung*)
4 dry red chillies (*sookhi lal mirch*)
½ tsp turmeric powder (*haldi*)
2 tbsp poppy seeds (*khus khus*)
1 tsp carom seeds (*ajwain*)
½ tsp cumin seeds (*jeera*)
10 peppercorns (*saboot kali mirch*)
1 tsp fennel seeds (*saunf*)
4 star anise (*chakri phool*)
1½ tbsp coriander seeds (*saboot dhania*)

1. Dry roast in a pan, coconut, garlic, cinnamon, cloves, whole red chillies, turmeric powder, poppy seeds, carom seeds, cumin seeds, peppercorns, fennel seeds, star anise and coriander seeds for 1-2 minutes. Remove. Cool. Grind to a paste with ¾ cup of water.
2. Heat oil in a kadhai/wok, add onions cook till brown.
3. Add the prepared masala paste and cook for 2 minutes.
4. Add the chicken pieces and saute for 7- 8 minutes.
5. Add 2 cups of water and salt. Bring to a boil. Lower heat and cook covered for 5 minutes.
6. Add tamarind pulp, grated nutmeg and mix well. Cook for a minute.
7. Serve hot with steamed rice.

47

Rogan Josh

The best of Kashmiri cuisine: this curry has a thin and delicate gravy with the traditional taste created by the use of fennel and dry ginger.

Serves 4

½ kg mutton (lamb)
½ cup thick yogurt (*dahi*)
¼ tsp asafoetida (*hing*) powder
6 tbsp oil
½ tsp red chilli powder (*degi mirch*)
salt to taste

GRIND TOGETHER & SIEVE TO GET A FINE POWDER
1 tbsp ginger powder (*saunth*)
2 tsp fennel (*saunf*)
3-4 cloves (*laung*)
seeds of 3 brown cardamoms (*moti elaichi*)
2 tsp cumin seeds (*jeera*)
3-4 dry, red chillies

1. Wash and pat dry mutton on a kitchen towel.
2. Heat oil in a pressure cooker. Add hing.
3. Add dry meat and stir fry for 4-5 minutes or till the mutton turns dry, golden brown and gives a well fried look. There should be no water of the meat left.
4. Add degi mirch. Mix well.
5. Mix the curd with the sifted powdered masala.
6. Add this curd to the mutton. Add salt. Stir fry for 5-7 minutes till the curd blends well and turns dry.
7. Add 2 cups of water, pressure cook for 7 minutes on full flame. Reduce flame and cook for 5 minutes. Remove from fire and let the pressure drop by itself. Check for tenderness.
8. Serve hot with rice or roti.

48

Maharashtrian Toor Dal

A touch of sweet and sour ((jaggery and lemon) gives this delicious dal the distinctive touch of the food of Maharashtra.

Serves 2-3

½ cup pigeon pea split (*toor dal*)
¾ tsp salt, or to taste
½ tsp turmeric powder (*haldi*)
1 tbsp jaggery (*gur*)
1 tbsp lemon juice, or to taste

TADKA/TEMPERING
2 tbsp clarified butter (*ghee*)
a pinch of asafoetida (*hing*)
½ tsp mustard seeds (*rai*)
some curry leaves

1. Clean, wash toor dal. Soak dal in 1½ cups of water for half an hour. Drain.

2. Pressure cook dal with 2 cups water, salt and haldi on high flame till the first whistle and then simmer for 5 minutes. Remove from heat.

3. After the pressure drops, add gur and ½ cup water. Mix well. Simmer for 2- 3 minutes. Remove from heat. The consistency should be thick.

4. For tadka/tempering heat ghee, add hing and rai. Let it crackle and add curry leaves and immediately add it to the dal. Squeeze lemon juice on it. Check taste. Serve with rice.

Kerala Chicken Stew

The cuisine of Kerala reflects the beauty of the land – this boneless chicken stew has a sweetly delicious coconut gravy choc-a-bloc with fresh, colourful vegetables.

Serves 6

250 gm boneless chicken - cut into 2" square pieces
2 cups of any combination of sliced mixed vegetables - (mushrooms, baby corn, snow peas, French beans, cauliflower, carrots, potatoes and onion)
4 tsp oil
seeds of 6-8 green cardamoms (*chhoti elaichi*)
2½" stick of cinnamon stick (dalchini)
6-8 cloves (*laung*)
1 green chilli - deseeded & cut into half
2½" piece of ginger - thinly sliced
10-12 curry leaves (*curry patta*)
2 cups coconut milk
1 tsp salt
1 tsp black peppercorns (*saboot kali mirch*) - coarsely ground

1. Heat oil in a pan, add seeds of chhoti elaichi, dalchini and laung. Wait for a minute. Add green chilli, ginger and curry patta. Saute for 2 minutes.

2. Add potatoes, carrots and onions. Cover and cook for 4 minutes.

3. Add the remaining vegetables, then add the chicken and stir-fry for 4-5 minutes.

4. Lower the heat, add the coconut milk and 1½ cups of water. Simmer for 8-10 minutes or until the chicken is cooked and the gravy thickens.

5. Remove from the heat. Add salt and stir well.

6. Sprinkle with black pepper and serve with Appams or boiled rice.

Tips:

1. Always simmer the coconut milk on a very low heat without covering, to prevent from curdling.

2. Add the salt to the coconut milk right in the end, after it has been boiled to prevent from curdling.

51

Paneer Makhani

This classic makhani gravy is created out of pureed tomatoes, butter, milk, cream and ground cashews – a paneer dish fit for a five-star banquet.

Serves 4

250 gm paneer - cut into 1" long pieces
¼ cup cashewnuts (*kaju*)
5 large (500 gm) tomatoes - each cut into 4 pieces
2 tbsp desi ghee or butter and 2 tbsp oil
4-5 flakes garlic and 1" piece ginger - ground to a paste (1½ tsp ginger-garlic paste)
1 tbsp dry fenugreek leaves (*kasoori methi*)
1 tsp tomato ketchup
½ tsp cumin seeds (*jeera*)
2 tsp coriander (*dhania*) powder
½ tsp garam masala
1 tsp salt, or to taste
½ tsp red chilli powder, preferably degi mirch
½ cup water, ½-1 cup milk, approx.
½ cup cream (optional)

1. Soak kaju in a little warm water for 10-15 minutes.
2. Drain kaju. Grind in a mixer to a very smooth paste using about 2 tbsp water.
3. Boil tomatoes in ½ cup water. Simmer for 4-5 minutes on low heat till tomatoes turn soft. Remove from fire & cool. Grind the tomatoes along with the water to a smooth puree.
4. Heat oil and ghee or butter in a kadhai. Reduce heat. Add jeera. When it turns golden, add ginger-garlic paste.
5. When paste starts to change colour add the above tomato puree & cook till dry.
6. Add kasoori methi & tomato ketchup.
7. Add masalas - dhania powder, garam masala, salt and red chilli powder. Mix well for a few seconds. Cook till oil separates.
8. Add cashew paste. Mix well for 2 minutes.
9. Add water. Boil. Simmer on low heat for 4-5 minutes. Reduce heat.
10. Add the paneer cubes. Remove from fire. Keep aside to cool for about 5 minutes.
11. Add enough milk to the cold paneer masala to get a thick curry, mix gently. (Remember to add milk only after the masala is no longer hot, to prevent the milk from curdling. After adding milk, heat curry on low heat.)
12. Heat on low heat, stirring continuously till just about to boil.
13. Add cream, keeping the heat very low and stirring continuously. Remove from fire immediately and transfer to a serving dish. Serve hot.

Variation:

For dakshini tadka, heat 1 tbsp oil. Add ½ tsp rai. After 30 seconds add 4- 5 curry leaves. Stir. Remove from fire. Add a pinch of red chilli powder and pour over the hot paneer makhani in the dish.

Quick Butter Chicken

Marinated chicken is cooked till tender, then simmered in a rich gravy made from pureed tomatoes, butter, cream and cashew paste. Degi mirch (paprika) gives a beautiful red colour, enhancing the appetising look.

Serves 4

1 medium sized chicken (800 gm) - cut into 12 pieces
6 tbsp oil

MARINADE
1 tbsp garlic paste or 8-10 flakes of garlic - crushed to a paste
1 tsp ginger paste or ½" piece of ginger - crushed to a paste
1 tbsp dry fenugreek leaves (*kasoori methi*)
½ tsp black salt (*kala namak*), ¾ tsp salt
1 tsp garam masala
few drops of orange red colour

MAKHANI GRAVY
½ kg (6-7) tomatoes or 2 cups ready-made tomato puree
2 tbsp butter, 2-3 tbsp oil
1 bay leaf (*tej patta*)
2 tbsp ginger-garlic paste or 1" piece of ginger & 16-18 flakes of garlic - crushed to a paste
4 tbsp cashewnuts (*kaju*)
¾ tsp kashmiri laal mirch or degi mirch
1 cup milk, 2 tbsp cream
½ tsp garam masala, 1 tsp salt, or to taste
1 tsp tandoori masala (optional)
¼ tsp sugar or to taste

1. Soak kaju in hot water for 15 minutes, drain and grind to a very fine paste with a little water in a mixer.

2. Wash the chicken well. Pat dry chicken with a clean kitchen napkin.

3. For the marinade, mix garlic & ginger paste, kasoori methi, kala namak, salt, garam masala and colour. Rub the chicken with this mixture. Keep aside for 15 minutes in the fridge.

4. Heat 6 tbsp oil in a kadhai, add marinated chicken, cook on high heat for 7- 8 minutes, stirring all the time. Reduce heat & cook covered for 10-15 minutes or till tender. Remove from fire. Keep aside.

5. To prepare the makhani gravy, boil water in a pan. Add tomatoes to boiling water. Boil for 3-4 minutes. Remove from water and peel. Let it cool down. Grind blanched tomatoes to a smooth puree. Keep aside.

6. Heat butter and oil together in a kadhai. Add tej patta. Stir for a few seconds. Add ginger and garlic paste, cook until liquid evaporates and the paste just changes colour.

7. Add pureed tomatoes or ready-made puree, degi mirch and sugar. Cook until the puree turns very dry and oil starts to float on top.

8. Add prepared kaju paste, stir for a few seconds on medium heat till fat separates. Lower the heat. Add about 1 cup of water to get the desired gravy. Add salt. Bring to a boil, stirring constantly.

9. Add cooked chicken. Cover and simmer for 5-7 minutes till the gravy turns to a bright colour. Reduce heat. Add milk on very low heat and bring to a boil, stirring continuously. Keep stirring for 1-2 minutes on low heat till you get the desired thickness of the gravy.

10. Remove from fire and stir in cream, stirring continuously. Add garam masala and tandoori masala. Stir. Garnish with 1 tbsp of fresh cream, slit green chillies and coriander. Serve hot with nan.

Note on blanching tomatoes :
To skin tomatoes, cut a small shallow X on the bottom, put in a bowl and pour boiling water on them to cover. Keep for 3 minutes and then plunge into cold water. The skins will slip off easily. You can also put the 'X' marked tomatoes in a micro proof bowl without water. 3 tomatoes need to be microwaved for 2½ minutes.

Sindhi Curry

A medley of vegetables in a well seasoned tangy tomato gravy thickened with gram flour.

Serves 4

500 gm tomatoes
3 tbsp oil
1½ tsp mustard seeds (*rai*)
1 tsp cumin seeds (*jeera*)
½ cup gram flour (*besan*)
1 potato - chopped, 8 green chillies
1 long, thin brinjal - chopped
3-4 guwar or french beans - chopped
2 drumsticks - cut into 3" pieces
10-12 lady fingers - each cut into 2 pieces
& fried in oil
½ tsp turmeric powder (*haldi*)
2 tsp red chilli powder
6 kokums or a lemon-size ball of tamarind
(*imli*) - soaked in ½ cup water
2 tbsp finely chopped coriander leaves
1½ tsp salt, or to taste

1. Boil tomatoes in 4 cups water for 3-4 minutes. Peel and puree in a mixer. Keep aside.
2. Heat 3 tbsp oil in a saucepan. Add mustard seeds and cumin seeds. Add gram flour and roast over medium flame for 4-5 minutes till golden brown. Remove from heat. Add tomatoes and 4 cups of water.
3. Mix well. Heat again. When it begins to boil add all vegetables except lady's fingers.
4. Add haldi, red chillies and 2 cups water. Simmer for 10 min. Add kokums or tamarind pulp and boil for 5 minutes. Add salt, fried lady's fingers and coriander leaves.

dry dishes

Dry Dishes

Achaari Paneer

Pickling spices give a distinct personality – the rest of the flavours provide a harmonious balance – you will be proud of this presentation!

Serves 6

300 gm paneer - cut into 1½" cubes
2 capsicums - cut into 1" pieces
¾" piece ginger & 5-6 flakes garlic -
crushed to a paste (2 tsp)
1 cup curd - beat well till smooth in a mixer
4 tbsp oil
3 onions - chopped finely
4 green chillies - chopped
½ tsp turmeric (*haldi*) powder
1 tsp dried mango powder (*amchoor*) or
lemon juice to taste
¾ tsp garam masala
1 tsp salt or to taste
2-3 green chillies - cut lengthwise into 4
pieces
¼ cup milk
2-3 tbsp cream, optional

ACHAARI MASALA
2 tsp aniseeds (*saunf*)
1 tsp mustard seeds (*rai*)
a pinch of fenugreek seeds (*methi daana*)
½ tsp onion seeds (*kalonji*)
1 tsp cumin seeds (*jeera*)

1. Cut paneer into 1½" cubes.
2. Sprinkle ½ tsp haldi, a pinch of salt and ½ tsp red chilli powder on the paneer and capsicum pieces. Mix well. Keep aside for 10 minutes.
3. Collect all seeds of the achaari masala - saunf, rai, methi daana, kalonji and jeera together.
4. Crush garlic and ginger to a paste.
5. Heat 4 tbsp oil. Add the collected seeds together to the hot oil. Let them crackle for 1 minute or till jeera turns golden.
6. Add onions and chopped green chillies. Cook till onions turn golden.
7. Add haldi and garlic-ginger paste. Mix well.
8. Reduce heat. Beat curd with 2 tbsp water and a pinch of haldi till smooth. Add gradually and keep stirring. Add amchoor, garam masala and salt or to taste. Cook for 2-3 minutes on low heat till the curd dries up a little. (Do not make it very dry). Remove from fire and let it cool down.
9. At the time of serving, add milk and slit green chillies. Add capsicum. Boil on low heat for a minute, stirring continuously. Cook on low flame for 2-3 minutes.
10. Add cream and paneer and cook for 1-2 minutes on low flame. Serve.

Tawa Jhinga Masala

Ajwain, carom seeds and ginger elevate this prawn delicacy from the ordinary to a gourmet masterpiece. So easy to make too!

Serves 4

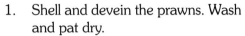

½ kg prawns - medium size
3 tbsp clarified butter (*ghee*)
1 tsp carom seeds (*ajwain*)
1 large onion - chopped (¾ cup)
2 green chillies - slit, deseed and chopped
½ tbsp chopped ginger
½ tsp red chilli powder
¼ cup chopped coriander
¾ cup ready-made tomato puree
salt to taste
¼ cup cream
1 tbsp lemon juice
½ tsp garam masala

1. Shell and devein the prawns. Wash and pat dry.
2. Heat ghee on a large tawa or a big pan, add prawns and saute over medium heat for 2-3 minutes till prawns change colour. Remove from tawa.
3. To the ghee in the same tawa, add ajwain and when it begins to crackle, add onions, green chillies and ginger, saute for 3 minutes.
4. Add tomato puree and cook until oil separates.
5. Add red chilli and coriander, *cook for ½ minute.*
6. Add prawns. Stir.
7. Add ceam, stirring continuously. Remove from fire Sprinkle lemon juice, garam masala, stir. Adjust the seasonings.
8. Remove to a dish and serve with any Indian bread of your choice.

Gobhi Fry

Cauliflower florets tossed in a delicious masala – everyone's favourite, at all times.

Serves 4

1 medium whole cauliflowers (500 gm) - cut into medium size florets with stalks

MASALA
4 tbsp oil
3 onions - chopped
seeds of 1 brown cardamom (*moti elaichi*)
3-4 peppercorns (*saboot kali mirch*)
2 cloves (*laung*)
3 tomatoes - roughly chopped
1" ginger - chopped
2 tbsp curd - beat well till smooth
½ tsp red chilli powder
½ tsp garam masala
½ tsp turmeric (*haldi*)
½ tsp dried mango powder (*amchoor*)
1 tsp salt, or to taste

1. Break the cauliflower into medium size florets, keeping the stalk intact. Wash & pat dry on a kitchen towel.
2. Heat oil in a kadhai for deep frying. Add all the cauliflower pieces and fry to a light brown colour. Remove from oil and keep aside.
3. Heat 4 tbsp oil in a clean kadhai. Add moti elaichi, saboot kali mirch and laung. After a minute, add chopped onion. Cook till onions turn golden brown.
4. Add chopped tomatoes and ginger. Cook for 4-5 minutes till they turn soft and masala turns little dry.
5. Add well beaten curd. Cook till masala turns reddish again.
6. Reduce heat. Add red chilli powder, garam masala, haldi, amchoor and salt. Cook for 1 minute. Add ½ cup water to get a thick masala. Boil. Cook for 1 minute on low flame. Keep aside.
7. At the time of serving, heat the masala. Add the fried cauliflower pieces to the masala and mix well on low heat for 2 minutes till the vegetable gets well blended with the masala. Serve hot.

Subziyaan Kali Mirch

Peppercorns and freshly ground pepper give an exciting lift to a colourful mix of crisp veggies and paneer – cream provides a luscious contrast.

Serves 5-6

3-4 tbsp butter, ¼ tsp peppercorns
2 tbsp grated ginger
1 onion - sliced
1 tsp salt, or to taste
1 tsp freshly ground pepper (grind or crush
few peppercorns (*kali mirch*) coarsely in a
spice grinder or on a *chakla belan*)
2-3 tbsp thick cream

VEGETABLES
100 gm paneer - cut into 4 and then cut into
thin long pieces
1 long, firm tomato
1 small capsicum, 5-6 French beans
1 carrot, 1 potato
1 tbsp lemon juice (adjust to taste)

1. Cut tomato into 4 and then cut into thin long pieces.
2. Cut capsicum into thin fingers.
3. Chop french beans into ¼" pieces (about ½ cup). Cut potato into 1" pieces. Cut carrot into round slices.
4. Boil 2 cups water with ¾ tsp salt & ½ tsp sugar. Add carrots and beans after the water boils. Boil for just 1-2 minutes till crisp-tender. Refresh in cold water. Strain. Keep aside.
5. Deep fry potatoes in a kadhai to a golden brown colour on medium heat and check that they get cooked on frying.

6. Heat butter on medium flame. (If the heat is too much, the butter will burn). Add peppercorns and wait for a minute. Add grated ginger. Fry on medium heat till slightly brown.
7. Add onions. Stir till golden.
8. Add beans, carrot, salt and pepper. Stir fry for 2 minutes.
9. Lower heat, add tomatoes. Cook covered for 2 minutes.
10. Add capsicum, paneer, fried potatoes and cream. Mix and remove from fire. Add lemon juice to taste. Sprinkle pepper and serve.

Kadhai Murg

The coating sauce made from tomatoes is enriched with cream and enlivened with fenugreek and coriander – wrap the sauce around the chicken pieces and please the crowds!

Serves 4-6

1 medium sized (800 gm) chicken - cut into 12 pieces
1 tbsp coriander seeds (*saboot dhania*)
3 whole, dry red chillies
6-7 tbsp oil
½ tsp fenugreek seeds (*methi daana*)
3 large onions - cut into slices
15-20 flakes garlic - crushed & chopped
1" piece of ginger - crushed to a paste
4 large tomatoes - chopped
½ cup ready-made tomato puree or ¾ cup home-made puree
1 tsp red chilli powder
1 tsp ground coriander (*dhania powder*)
2 tsp salt, or to taste
¼ tsp dried mango powder (*amchoor*)
½ tsp garam masala
½ cup chopped green coriander
1 capsicum - cut into slices
1" piece ginger - cut into match sticks
1-2 green chillies - cut into long slices
½ cup cream, optional

1. Put saboot dhania (coriander seeds) and whole red chillies on a tawa. Keep on fire and roast lightly till it just starts to change colour. Do not make them brown. Remove from fire.

2. Crush the saboot dhania on a chakla-belan (rolling board and pin) to split the seeds. Keep red chillies whole. Keep aside.

3. Heat oil in a kadhai. Reduce heat. Add methi daana and the roasted whole red chillies and stir for a few seconds till methi daana turns golden.

4. Add onion and cook on medium heat till light brown.

5. Add garlic and stir for 1 minute.

6. Add ginger paste.

7. Add the crushed saboot dhania, red chilli powder and dhania powder.

8. Add chicken and bhuno for 10 minutes on high flame, stirring well so that chicken attains a nice golden brown colour.

9. Add chopped tomatoes. Cook for 4-5 minutes.

10. Add salt, amchoor and garam masala. Cover and cook for 15-20 minutes or till tender, stirring occasionally.

11. Add tomato puree & chopped green coriander. Cook for 5 minutes.

12. Add the capsicum, ginger match sticks and green chilli slices. Mix well.

13. Reduce heat. Add cream. Mix well for 2-3 minutes and remove from fire. Serve hot.

Keema Matar

One can never get tired of this satisfying, delicious and hearty family favourite.

Serves 2-3

5-6 tbsp oil/ghee
250 gm mutton mince (*keema*) -
washed and drained well
¾ cup shelled peas (*matar*) or 1 small
capsicum- chopped
4-5 cloves (*laung*)
1" stick cinnamon (*dalchini*)
4-5 peppercorns (*saboot kali mirch*)
1 large onion - chopped (1 cup)
5-6 flakes garlic - finely chopped
½" piece ginger - finely chopped
1 large tomato - chopped (1 cup)
1 tsp salt
¾ tsp red chilli powder (adjust to taste)
¾ tsp garam masala powder
½ tsp turmeric (*haldi*) powder

1. Wash the mince in a strainer. Press to drain out the water well.

2. Heat oil/ghee in a pressure cooker. Add laung, dalchini and saboot kali mirch. Fry for 1 minute.

3. Add chopped onions, ginger and garlic. Fry till onions turn rich brown in colour.

4. Add keema. Stir fry for 4- 5 minutes.

5. Add tomatoes, all seasonings and cook very well till oil separates.

6. Add peas or capsicum. Mix well.

7. Add ¾ cup water. Close the pressure cooker and give 3 whistles.

8. Open the cooker when the pressure drops. Cook and dry the keema as much as you like (some people like it absolutely dry and some like it wettish).

9. Garnish with chopped tomatoes and fresh coriander. Serve hot.

rice & paranthas

Rice & Paranthas

Jalpari Biryani

Biryani made with layers of basmati rice and spiced lotus stem (bhein) sprinkled with fresh mint and mace (javitri). Use fresh and tender bhein for best flavour.

Serves 4

125 gm bhein or lotus stem (*kamal kakri*)

RICE
1 cup basmati rice - soaked for 20-30 minutes
3-4 chhoti elaichi (green cardamoms)
1 moti elaichi (black cardamom)
½" stick dalchini (cinnamon)
½ tsp salt, 4 cups water

MINT PASTE *(grind together to a paste)*
2-3 tbsp mint leaves (poodina)
4 tbsp coriander chopped, 1 green chilli

MASALA
3 onions, 1" piece ginger
½ tsp red chilli powder
1 tbsp kishmish (raisin)
½ cup curd - well beaten & mixed with
¼ cup water

OTHER INGREDIENTS
2 tbsp chopped mint leaves
2 onions - sliced and deep fried till brown
½ cup curd - well beaten
2 pinches of *javitri* - crushed and powdered
seeds of 2 green cardamoms
(*chhoti elaichi*) - powdered

1. Peel bhein. Cut into thin diagonal slices and soak slices in water. Keep aside.
2. Prepare mint paste by grinding all the ingredients of the paste together.
3. Grind onions, ginger and red chilli powder together to a paste.
4. Heat 1 karchhi (4-5 tbsp oil) in a handi or a heavy bottomed pan. Add the onion paste. Cook on low flame till light brown & oil separates.
5. Add kishmish & stir for ½ a minute.
6. Reduce flame. Add beaten curd mixed with a little water, stirring continuously to prevent curd from curdling. Stir till masala turns thick.
7. Drain bhein and add to the masala. Add 1 tsp salt. Bhuno for 4-5 minutes.
8. Add 1 cup water. Cover with a tight fitting lid and cook on low flame for 15 minutes or till soft. The bhein should not taste raw, although it may taste a little hard.
9. Add mint paste. Bhuno for 5-7 minutes, remove from fire and keep aside. Keep bhein aside.
10. To prepare the rice, boil 4 cups water with all the saboot garam masala & salt.
11. Drain the soaked rice and add to boiling water. Keep checking and feeling a grain of rice in between the finger and thumb to see if it is done. Boil on medium flame for 7-8 minutes till the rice is nearly done. Take care to see that the rice is not over cooked.

12. Strain rice in a rice strainer or colander. Keep aside uncovered for 10 minutes. Then spread the rice in a big tray.
13. Deep fry 2 sliced onions to a crisp brown colour. Keep aside.
14. Beat ½ cup curd. Add crushed and powdered javitri and chhoti elaichi to the curd. Keep aside.
15. Finely chop 2 tbsp mint leaves and keep aside.
16. To assemble the biryani, put half the vegetable with the masala in a handi.

17. Spread half the rice over it.
18. Spoon half the flavoured curd over it.
19. Sprinkle some fried onions and chopped mint leaves.
20. Repeat the masala vegetable and the other layers.
21. Cover the handi. Seal with atta dough and keep on dum for 15-20 minutes in a slow oven (100°C). Break the seal just before serving.

Makai Khichdi

Simple and wholesome with plenty of flavour and eye-appeal – enjoy the sweetness of corn in this delicious khichdi.

Serves 2

1¼ cups rice
3 tbsp ghee or butter
a pinch of asafoetida (*hing*)
2" piece of ginger - chopped
2-3 green chillies - remove seeds & chop finely
3 tsp salt
2 tbsp chopped coriander leaves
1 tsp lemon juice
1 tsp turmeric powder (*haldi*)
1 tsp cumin seeds (*jeera*)
1 cup corn kernels (*bhutte ke daane*)
3½ cups water for cooking rice

1. Wash and soak the rice for half an hour.
2. Heat ghee in a saucepan. Add jeera. Cook till it starts to change colour.
3. Add hing and then add chopped ginger, chopped green chillies and haldi. Mix well and cook for 2-3 minutes.
4. Add cooked corn & 3½ cups water and bring to a boil. Add rice, salt, coriander and lemon juice, mix and cook covered on slow flame till rice is cooked and the khichdi is of the right consistency.
5. Garnish with garam masala & red chilli powder. Serve hot with yogurt, papad and pickle of your choice.

Tip: Consistency of khichdi is a matter of personal preference. If you want khichdi to be runny, add a little more water.

Hyderabadi Biryani Khaas

Rice and chicken are cooked separately, and then they are layered together along with fried onions. The pot is tightly sealed and steamed on low heat to allow all the flavours to blend.

Serves 6-8

RICE
2 cups uncooked long grain
basmati rice, 1 tbsp oil
2 bay leaves (*tej patta*), 1½ tsp salt

FOR THE CHICKEN
1 chicken (700-800 gm) - cut into 12 pieces
4 large onions - chopped
1½ tbsp ginger-garlic paste
2 large tomatoes - chopped
1 cup thick yogurt (*curd*), 5-6 tbsp oil
1 tsp red chilli powder, salt to taste

GARNISHING
1 cup sliced onions - fried till crisp and
brown (2-3 large onions)
½ cup mint leaves (*poodina*)
few strands saffron (*kesar*) soaked in
1 tsp water and 2 drops kewra essence

FLAVOURING MASALA
1½ tsp cumin (*jeera*)
3-4 green cardamoms (*chhoti elaichi*)
3-4 cloves (laung), 2" cinnamon (*dalchini*)
2-3 peppercorns (*saboot kali mirch*)
2 black cardamoms (*moti elaichi*)
¼ cup water

1. To cook the rice, boil 7 cups of water with tej patta, salt, & oil. Add the rice and cook till almost tender. Strain and spread the drained rice on a wide tray. Run a fork through the rice to let the steam escape.

2. For chicken, heat oil in a kadhai/ wok. Add onions. Stir fry till brown.

3. Add ginger-garlic paste. Mix well.

4. Add tomatoes. Cook till dry. Add curd. Stir for 1 minute. Add salt, chilli powder & chicken. Bhuno for 8 minutes. Add 1 cup water Cook till tender. Remove from fire.

5. Grind all the ingredients for the flavouring masala in a blender to a paste. Strain it through a sieve. Keep liquid masala aside.

6. For assembling the biryani, take a large heavy-bottomed pan, sprinkle some curry of the chicken at the bottom. Spread some of the rice. Place ½ the chicken pieces on it and wet the rice with some curry.

7. Sprinkle some of the fried onion and poodina on it. Sprinkle 2-3 tbsp liquid flavouring masala.

8. Repeat by adding rice, then chicken, followed by poodina and fried onions and flavouring masala. Finish with a top layer of rice sprinkled with fried onions, poodina, flavouring masala and kesar mixture. Mix slightly.

9. Cover the pan with a tight fitting lid and seal the lid with dough. Place the pan on fire with a tawa underneath to reduce the heat to minimum for ½ hour before serving.

Kashmiri Gosht Pulao

Unlike a biryani, a pulao does not need layering since the rice cooks in the mutton stock and absorbs all the flavours fully.

Serves 5-6

500 gm mutton, preferably mutton with very little bones - wash well
2½ cups basmati rice - washed and soaked for 30 minutes
5-6 tbsp ghee, 2 onions - sliced
3 green chillies-chopped, 1 tsp ginger paste
1 cup yogurt (*dahi*), 3 tsp salt

KHUS KHUS PASTE
1½ tbsp poppy seeds (*khus-khus*) - soaked in warm water for ½ hour
seeds of 8 green cardamoms (*chhoti elaichi*) and 2 black cardamoms (*moti elaichi*)
1½ tbsp fennel (*saunf*) powder
1½ tsp cumin seeds (*jeera*)
8-10 peppercorns (*saboot kali mirch*)
8 cloves (*laung*)
2" stick of cinnamon (*dalchini*)

1. Wash rice and preferably soak for 30 minutes.
2. Put mutton, 1 tsp salt and 5 cups water in a pressure cooker. Pressure cook to give 4-5 whistles. Reduce heat and keep on low heat for 5 minutes. Mutton should be tender. (The number of whistles will depend on the quality of mutton). Remove.
3. Grind all ingredients for the khus khus paste grind together to a fine paste in a mixer. Keep aside.
4. Heat ghee in a heavy-bottomed pan. Add sliced onion. Fry till brown.
5. Add ginger paste and green chillies. Mix well.
6. Add mutton pieces (without the stock). Add the freshly made khus khus paste to the mutton. Mix well. Fry for 5-6 minutes.
7. Measure the mutton stock and add water if required to make it to 4½ cups.
8. Add dahi, rice and 2 tsp salt. Add 4½ cups stock. Boil.
9. Cover and cook on low heat till rice is well cooked and the water dries up. Separate with a fork . Serve hot.

Kerala Parantha

A flaky parantha from the Malabar coast – a delightful addition to the immense variety and range in the world of breads.

Makes 6

450 gm flour (*maida*)
a pinch of soda-bi-carb (*mitha soda*)
2 eggs
150 ml (2/3 cup) milk
2½ tsp sugar
1 tsp salt
4 tbsp oil
7 tbsp butter
some flour (*maida*), to dust
ghee to shallow fry

1. Break the eggs in a bowl, add milk, sugar, salt and oil, whisk well.
2. Sieve flour and with soda bi-carb through a fine sieve (channi) into a big bowl (paraat).
3. Make a bay in the sieved flour, pour the egg and milk mixture in it and start mixing gradually. When fully mixed, knead to make a soft dough, cover with a moist cloth and keep aside for 30 minutes.
4. Divide dough into 6 equal portions and make balls. Flatten each with a belan (rolling pin) into a round disc. Grease the rolling surface with oil, place the flattened dough and stretch evenly on all sides until it is very thin (approx. 15-inch diameter). Apply melted butter over the entire surface, dust with flour, hold from two ends and gather ensuring there are many folds. Place the dough on the table and roll to make a pedha (ball) and then flatten slightly. Keep aside for 5 minutes. Flatten each pedha with a belan (rolling pin) into a round disc (approx. 9-inch diameter), dusting with flour while rolling.
5. Place Paratha on a heated tawa/ griddle and cook on one side, turn side pour melted ghee all round and shallow fry both sides over low heat until golden brown. Remove and serve immediately.

Anda Parantha

Slip an egg into the pocket of a potato-stuffed parantha and let it set – a fantastic treat for hungry tummies!

Serves 4

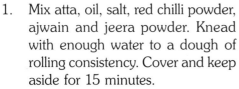

DOUGH
2 cups whole wheat flour (*atta*)
2 tbsp oil
¾ tsp salt, ½ tsp red chilli powder
½ tsp carom seeds (*ajwain*)
½ tsp cumin powder (*jeera*)

OTHER INGREDIENTS
4 eggs
2 potatoes - boiled and mashed
salt to taste, ½ tsp red chilli powder
½ tsp garam masala
oil or ghee for frying

1. Mix atta, oil, salt, red chilli powder, ajwain and jeera powder. Knead with enough water to a dough of rolling consistency. Cover and keep aside for 15 minutes.
2. Mix potatoes with salt, red chilli powder and garam masala.
3. Make 4 balls from the dough. Roll out a ball to a diameter of 5" like the size of a poori.
4. Put a heaped tbsp of mashed potatoes (about ¼ of the mixture) in the centre. Collect the sides of the rolled out dough to cover the filling.

5. Flatten the stuffed ball slightly and press over dry flour. Roll out to a slightly thick parantha.
6. Carefully pick up the parantha and put it on a hot griddle (tawa). When the underside is cooked, turn to cook the other side. Smear some oil or ghee on the parantha. Trickle some oil on the sides too, around the edges. Turn the parantha to make it light golden.
7. When the parantha is almost done, shut off the fire. Make a 3-4" slit, a little away from the edge of the parantha. Open up the parantha from the slit with the help of a knife to get a pocket.
8. Break a whole egg in a small bowl. Put the egg all together in the pocket of the parantha. Return to low heat and let the egg in the parantha cook for 2-3 minutes on low heat. Remove parantha from tawa when it turns crisp and golden brown on both sides. Serve hot.

Tandoori Keema Parantha

Tasty and juicy chicken keema makes mouth-watering layers in this incredibly flaky parantha cooked in a tandoor or oven.

Makes 6

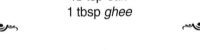

FILLING
250 gm chicken mince (*keema*)
2 tbsp oil
1 onion - chopped finely
2 tsp finely chopped ginger
1 tsp salt
1 tsp coriander (*dhania*) powder
½ tsp red chilli powder
½ tsp garam masala
2 green chillies - chopped
1 tbsp finely chopped fresh coriander
1 tbsp dried fenugreek leaves (*kasoori methi*)

DOUGH
2 cups whole wheat flour (*atta*)
½ tsp salt
1 tbsp *ghee*

1. To prepare the dough, sift flour and salt. Rub in 1 tbsp ghee. Add enough water to make a dough. Keep aside for 30 minutes.
2. To prepare the filling, heat 2 tbsp of oil and stir fry the chopped onions until brown.
3. Add mince and ginger and cook for 3-4 minutes.
4. Add salt, dhania powder, red chilli powder and garam masala. Fry for 1-2 minutes. Cook covered on low heat for about 5 minutes, till the mince is cooked.
5. Add green chillies and 1 tbsp finely chopped coriander . If there is any water, uncover and dry the mince on fire. Keep the filling aside.
6. Divide the dough into 6 equal parts. Shape into round balls.
7. Flatten each ball, roll out each into a round of 5" diameter.
8. Spread 1 tsp ghee. Then spread 1-2 tbsp of filling all over.
9. Make a slit, starting from the centre till any one end.
10. Start rolling from the slit, to form an even cone.
11. Keeping the cone upright, press slightly.
12. Roll out, applying pressure only at the centre. Do not roll or press too much on the sides, otherwise the layers of parantha do not separate after cooking.
13. Sprinkle some kasoori methi and press with a rolling pin (belan).
14. Apply water on the back side of the parantha and stick carefully in a heated tandoor or place in a preheated oven in a greased tray.
15. Remove after a few minutes. Spread some ghee, serve hot.

Lachha Poodina Parantha

The flavour of mint is crusted right on top of this so-easy-to-make flaky parantha, making every bite a pure delight!

Makes 6

4 tbsp freshly chopped or
dry mint leaves (*poodina*)
2 cups whole wheat flour (*atta*)
1 tsp carom seeds (*ajwain*)
2 tbsp oil, ½ tsp salt
½ tsp red chilli powder

1. Mix atta with all ingredients except poodina. Add enough water to make a dough of rolling consistency.
2. Make walnut-sized balls. Roll out to make a thick chappati.
3. Spread 1 tsp of ghee all over. Cut a slit from the outer edge till the centre.
4. Start rolling from the slit to form a cone.
5. Keeping the cone upright, press cone gently.
6. Roll out to a thick roti. Sprinkle poodina. Press with the belan (rolling pin).
7. Cook on a tawa, frying on both sides or apply some water on the back side of the parantha and stick it in a hot tandoor. Serve hot.

Southern Tomato Rice

Cooked rice is tossed in a spicy tomato base till it soaks up all the flavours.

Serves 4

1 cup basmati rice
4 small tomatoes - ground to a puree
in a mixi
2-3 onions - chopped
¼ tsp turmeric powder (*haldi*)
1½ tsp salt or to taste
1 tsp red chilli powder
¼ tsp asafoetida (*hing*) powder

TEMPERING (*CHOWNK*)
3 tbsp oil, 1 tsp mustard seeds (*sarson*)
1 tbsp bengal gram dal (*channe ki dal*)
few curry leaves

1. Clean & wash rice. Boil 5-6 cups water in a large pan. Add rice. Cook till done.

2. Strain the rice in a colander (big metal strainer). Keep aside to cool by spreading the rice in a big tray.

3. Heat oil in a kadhai. Reduce flame. Add sarson & dal. Cook on very low flame till dal changes colour.

4. Add curry leaves & onions. Fry till onions turn light brown.

5. Add tomato puree.

6. Add haldi, salt & red chilli powder.

7. Cook on low flame till the dal turns soft & the tomatoes turn absolutely dry & oil separates. Add hing powder.

8. Separate the rice grains with a fork & add to the tomatoes. Stir carefully till well mixed. Serve hot.

Chutneys, Raitas & Achaar

Baingan Ka Raita

Cool and pure yogurt is contrasted with tingling mustard seeds, curry leaves and red chillies – with slices of fried brinjals stirred in, this makes the perfect raita.

Serves 4-6

1 small thin, long aubergine (*baingan*)
1 tsp chaat masala
2 cups yogurt (*dahi*)
1 tsp salt, oil to shallow fry

FOR TEMPERING (*TADKA*)
1 tbsp oil
1 tbsp black mustard (*sarson*) seeds
6-8 curry leaves (*curry patta*)
2 whole dry red chillies (*saboot sookhi lal mirch*)

1. Wash and cut the baingan into thin round slices.
2. Heat the oil in a non stick frying pan; add baingan, fry till light brown. Sprinkle chaat masala. Remove.
3. Beat dahi with salt well. Pour into a serving bowl. Add baingan. Mix gently.
4. For the tempering, heat the oil and all ingredients of the tadka, wait for a minute. Immediately pour over the yogurt. Serve chilled.

Chicken Achaar

All the traditional pickling spices are used – but when the main ingredient is chicken, you have something fantastically different!

Serves 8

½ kg boneless chicken - cut into
1" pieces
1 tsp red chilli powder
½ tsp turmeric (*haldi*)
1 tsp salt
1½ tbsp ginger paste, 1½ tbsp garlic paste
1½ cups mustard oil
½ tsp asafoetida (*hing*)
1 big onion - chopped (¾ cup)
1 cup malt vinegar (200 ml)

SPICES FOR ACHHAR
seeds of 1 black cardamom (*moti elaichi*) &
seeds of 2 green cardamom (*chhoti elaichi*)
- powdered, ¾ tsp salt
2 tsp fennel seeds (*saunf*) - powdered
½ tbsp black cumin seeds (*shah jeera*)
½ tsp fenugreek seeds (*methi daana*)
1¼ tsp mustard seeds (*rai*)
2 bay leaves (*tej patta*)

1. Mix chicken with red chilli powder, haldi, salt, half of ginger and garlic pastes. Keep aside for 30 minutes.
2. Heat oil in a kadhai/wok to a smoking point, reduce to medium heat and deep fry the marinated chicken pieces for 2-3 minutes. Remove chicken and strain the oil.
3. Collect all the achaar spices together and keep aside.
4. Heat the strained oil in a separate kadhai/wok, add hing, stir for 15 seconds, add onions and deep fry until golden brown. Then add the remaining ginger and garlic pastes, stir for 2 minutes. Add the collected achaar spices and stir for ½ minutes.
5. Add vinegar. Bring to a boil, add the fried chicken & stir over high heat for 3-4 minutes. Remove & cool.
6. Transfer to a sterilized earthenware or glass jar, secure with muslin cloth around the opening of the jar and leave it in the sun or in a warm place for 2 days. Remove the muslin and cover with a lid. Consume within 60 days.

Note:

(i) Ensure all moisture is removed from the chicken before pickling. The presence of moisture induces fungal growth & reduces shelf life.

(ii) For Chaamp achaar (lamb chops), follow the recipe above, except use 100 gm each of the ginger and garlic pastes and 4 cups of malt vinegar. Also, the lamb must be boiled, until tender, before marination.

(iii) For Pork, the meat has to be boiled over an extended period—until tender. The rest of the recipe is the same as above.

Prawn Balchao

Serve this at room temperature as a very special achaar – or serve hot as an exclusive and elegant side dish – either way you have a winner!

Serves 12

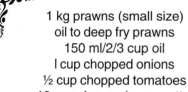
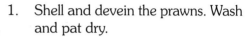

1 kg prawns (small size)
oil to deep fry prawns
150 ml/2/3 cup oil
l cup chopped onions
½ cup chopped tomatoes
10 curry leaves (*curry patta*)
2½ tsp sugar
salt to taste

PASTE
20 whole red chillies
4" stick of cinnamon (*dalchini*)
15 green cardamom (*chhoti elaichi*)
15 cloves (*laung*)
1 tsp peppercorns (*saboot kali mirch*)
1 tsp cumin seeds (*jeera*)
1 tbsp chopped garlic
3 tbsp chopped ginger
¾ cup malt vinegar
1 tsp sarson seeds (rai)

1. Shell and devein the prawns. Wash and pat dry.
2. Heat oil in a kadhai and deep fry prawns for 2 minutes. Remove.
3. Grind all ingredients of paste to a smooth paste in a blender.
4. Heat oil in a kadhai or wok, add onions and saute over medium heat until golden brown.
5. Add tomatoes, stir for 2- 3 minutes.
6. Add the paste and cook for 5-6 minutes.
7. Add prawns and stir for 2 minutes.
8. Add curry leaves and sugar, stir. Add salt to taste. Serve at room temperature.

Dahi Poodina Chutney

This pretty green-tinted chutney is hot (with green chillies) and cool (with yogurt), both at the same time!

Serves 6

1½ cups curd - hang for 15 minutes
a pinch of black salt (*kala namak*)
¼ tsp roasted cumin seeds (*bhuna jeera*)
salt to taste
1 tsp oil

GREEN PASTE
½ cup mint (*poodina*)
½ cup green coriander (*hara dhania*)
2 green chillies
½ onion
2 flakes garlic

1. Hang curd in a muslin cloth for 15 minutes. Keep aside.
2. Wash coriander and mint leaves.
3. Grind coriander, mint, green chillies, onion and garlic with a little water to a green paste.
4. Beat hung curd well till smooth.
5. To the hung curd, add the green paste, oil, kala namak, bhuna jeera and salt to taste.

Onion Garlic Chutney

Tamarind, jaggery and roasted peanuts add new dimensions to taste!

Makes ½ cup

1 large onion - chopped roughly
4-5 flakes of garlic
1-2 whole dry red chillies, deseeded
2 tbsp roasted peanuts
1 tbsp oil
1 small piece of jaggery
½ tsp salt or to taste
2 tbsp tamarind pulp

1. Heat ½ tbsp oil in a pan add onion, chillies and garlic. Cook till onions turn soft. Cool.

2. Put the onion-chilli-garlic and all the other ingredient in a mixer and grind to a smooth paste.

3. Heat the remaining oil & pour over the chutney Mix.

desserts

Desserts

Pista Kesar Kulfi

The perfect recipe that works every time – stock your freezer with this popular dessert.

Serves 6

1 kg (5 cups) full cream milk
a few strands of saffron (*kesar*)
¼ cup sugar, 2 tbsp cornflour
75 gm fresh *khoa* - grated & mashed
slightly (¾ cup grated)
1 tbsp pistachio (*pista*) - very finely cut
1 tbsp almonds - very finely cut
3-4 crushed green cardamoms (*chhoti elaichi*)

1. Dissolve cornflour in 1 cup milk and keep aside.

2. Boil the rest of the milk with kesar in a kadhai till it is reduced to half in quantity, for about 25-30 minutes on medium fire, scraping the sides.

3. Add sugar and cornflour paste. Boil. Cook for 2-3 minutes more till the sugar is well dissolved.

4. Remove from fire. Cool slightly.

5. Add khoya, almonds, pista and crushed elaichi.

6. Fill the mixture in the kulfi moulds. Freeze for 6-8 hours or overnight.

Aam Ki Phirni

Surprise your guests with this innovative interpretation of a very traditional dessert.

Serves 6

3½ cups (700 gm) milk at room temp.
1/3 cup *basmati* rice
1 large mango of good flavour (alphanso
or *langda*) - pureed in a mixer to get 1 cup
mango puree
1/3 cup sugar or to taste
4 almonds (*badaam*) - shredded
5-6 green pistachio (*pista*) - shredded
2 small silver leaves, optional
seeds of 1 green cardamom (*chhoti elaichi*)
- powdered

1. Soak rice of good quality for about an hour and then grind very fine with 4 to 5 tablespoonfuls of cold water. Dissolve the rice paste in ½ cup milk and make a thin paste.

2. Mix the rice paste with the remaining milk in a heavy bottomed kadhai. Keep on fire. Cook on medium heat, stirring continuously, till the mixture comes to a boil. Simmer for 5 minutes on low heat, stirring continuously till the mixture is of creamy consistency.

3. Add sugar and cardamom powder and stir.

4. Simmer till it is fully dissolved and then boil for 3-4 minutes.

5. Remove from fire. Let it cool. Mix well till creamy. Add mango puree and half of the shredded almonds and pistachios.

6. Pour the mixture into 6 small glass bowls.

7. Chill. Decorate each dish with a silver leaf, a few shredded nuts and rose petals.

Note: To avoid lumps, never add rice paste to hot milk. After adding rice paste to milk, keep on fire and stir continuously till phirni is ready.

Fruit should be added after the phirni cools down.

Badaam Ka Halwa

If you are looking for pure pleasure try this halwa! Almond paste and khoya sautéed in ghee, then cooked with sugar and milk.

Serves 4

150 gm (1 cup) almonds
200 gm *khoya* - grate or crumble
1 cup sugar
1 cup milk
15 gm (1 tbsp) clarified butter/*desi ghee*
seeds of 2 green cardamoms (*chhoti elaichi*) - powdered

1. Soak almonds in water for 2-3 hours or overnight. Remove peel and grind to a paste. Keep almond paste aside.
2. Heat ghee in a heavy-bottom pan.
3. Add khoya, cook on low heat for about 4-5 minutes, till light golden.
4. Add almond paste cook for about 4-5 minutes, till khoya becomes golden.
5. Add sugar. Stir for 3-4 minutes on low flame.
6. Add milk and elaichi powder. Cook till halwa leaves ghee, approx. 10 minutes. Garnish with almonds.

Malpuas

These pancakes are soaked in syrup, making them one of the best desserts for people with a sweet tooth. Prepare the batter at least one hour before frying the malpuas.

Gives 12-14 small malpuas

BATTER
1 cup flour (*maida*)
2 tbsp whole wheat flour (*atta*)
1 cup cream (*malai*)
½ cup milk (as much as required)
ghee for frying

SUGAR SYRUP
1 cup sugar
½ cup water
a few strands saffron or 1-2 drops yellow food colour
1-2 green cardamoms (*chhoti elaichi*) - powdered

1. Mix all the ingredients well so that no lumps remain. The batter should be a little thicker than a cake batter. It should be of a soft dropping consistency. A thin batter will spread.

2. Leave aside for 1-2 hours. (very essential)

3. Heat ghee in a nonstick frying pan.

4. With the help of a spoon drop a spoonful of batter in moderately hot ghee. Spread to get a small round malpua. Put as many (about 4-5) malpuas as the pan can hold.

5. Fry on both sides to golden brown. Drain & keep aside.

6. Mix sugar, water & all other ingredients for sugar syrup in a pan. Boil for 3-4 minutes to get one thread consistency syrup.

7. Drop malpuas in hot syrup, 2-3 at a time. Give 1-2 boils. Remove with a slotted spoon so that excess syrup is drained.

8. Place on a serving dish garnished with chopped almonds & pistas. Serve plain or with rabri or kheer.

Note: Malpuas can be fried in advance & kept without sugar syrup in an airtight box in the fridge for 1-2 days.

At the time of serving drop into hot sugar syrup, give 1-2 boils and serve hot.

Payasam

Fine vermicelli is cooked in ghee, sugar and milk then garnished with fried nuts and raisins.

Serves 6

4 cups milk
½ cup water
¾ cup sugar, or to taste
1 cup broken vermicelli (*seviyaan*)
2 tbsp *ghee*
a large pinch of saffron (*kesar*), optional
1 tbsp broken cashewnut pieces (*kaju tukda*)
2 tbsp raisins
3-4 cardamoms - powdered
a few drops rose essence

1. Heat ghee. Fry cashewnut pieces and raisins, remove, set aside.

2. Add seviyaan to the pan, fry to a light brown, add water, cook for just a minute, on low heat.
3. Now add the milk gradually, stirring.
4. Add sugar, continue to cook until payasam is quite thick. Remove from fire. Check sugar.
5. Add cardamom, nuts and raisins. Add rose essence, mix all of it, thoroughly. Serve hot or cold.

Note: You could add a large pinch of saffron along with milk while it is boiling, then drop rose essence.

GLOSSARY OF NAMES/TERMS

HINDI OR ENGLISH NAMES AS USED IN INDIA	ENGLISH NAMES AS USED IN USA/UK/ OTHER COUNTRIES
Aloo	Potatoes
Badaam	Almonds
Basmati rice	Fragrant Indian rice
Capsicum	Bell peppers
Chaawal, Chawal	Rice
Choti Elaichi	Green cardamom
Chilli powder	Red chilli powder, Cayenne pepper
Cornflour	Cornstarch
Coriander, fresh	Cilantro
Cream	Whipping cream
Dalchini	Cinnamon
Degi Mirch, Kashmiri Mirch	Paprika
Elaichi	Cardamom
Gajar	Carrots
Gobhi	Cauliflower
Hara Dhania	Cilantro/fresh or green coriander
Hari Mirch	Green hot peppers, green chillies, serrano peppers
Jeera Powder	Ground cumin seeds
Kaju	Cashewnuts
Khumb	Mushrooms
Kishmish	Raisins
Maida	All purpose flour, Plain flour
Makai, Makki	Corn
Matar	Peas
Mitha soda	Baking soda
Nimbu	Lemon
Paneer	Home made cheese made by curdling milk with vinegar or lemon juice. Fresh home made ricotta cheese can be substituted.
Pyaz, pyaaz	Onions
Red Chilli Flakes	Red pepper flakes
Saboot Kali Mirch	Peppercorns
Saunf	Fennel
Soda bicarb	Baking soda
Spring Onions	Green onions, Scallions
Suji	Semolina
Til	Sesame seeds
Toned Milk	Milk with 1% fat content

INTERNATIONAL CONVERSION GUIDE

These are not exact equivalents; they've been rounded-off to make measuring easier.

WEIGHTS & MEASURES

METRIC	IMPERIAL
15 g	½ oz
30 g	1 oz
60 g	2 oz
90 g	3 oz
125 g	4 oz (¼ lb)
155 g	5 oz
185 g	6 oz
220 g	7 oz
250 g	8 oz (½ lb)
280 g	9 oz
315 g	10 oz
345 g	11 oz
375 g	12 oz (¾ lb)
410 g	13 oz
440 g	14 oz
470 g	15 oz
500 g	16 oz (1 lb)
750 g	24 oz (1½ lb)
1 kg	30 oz (2 lb)

LIQUID MEASURES

METRIC	IMPERIAL
30 ml	1 fluid oz
60 ml	2 fluid oz
100 ml	3 fluid oz
125 ml	4 fluid oz
150 ml	5 fluid oz (¼ pint/1 gill)
190 ml	6 fluid oz
250 ml	8 fluid oz
300 ml	10 fluid oz (½ pint)
500 ml	16 fluid oz
600 ml	20 fluid oz (1 pint)
1000 ml	1¾ pints

CUPS & SPOON MEASURES

METRIC	IMPERIAL
1 ml	¼ tsp
2 ml	½ tsp
5 ml	1 tsp
15 ml	1 tbsp
60 ml	¼ cup
125 ml	½ cup
250 ml	1 cup

HELPFUL MEASURES

METRIC	IMPERIAL
3 mm	1/8 in
6 mm	¼ in
1 cm	½ in
2 cm	¾ in
2.5 cm	1 in
5 cm	2 in
6 cm	2½ in
8 cm	3 in
10 cm	4 in
13 cm	5 in
15 cm	6 in
18 cm	7 in
20 cm	8 in
23 cm	9 in
25 cm	10 in
28 cm	11 in
30 cm	12 in (1ft)

HOW TO MEASURE

When using the graduated metric measuring cups, it is important to shake the dry ingredients loosely into the required cup. Do not tap the cup on the table, or pack the ingredients into the cup unless otherwise directed. Level top of cup with a knife. When using graduated metric measuring spoons, level top of spoon with a knife. When measuring liquids in the jug, place jug on a flat surface, check for accuracy at eye level.

OVEN TEMPERATURE

These oven temperatures are only a guide. Always check the manufacturer's manual.

	°C (Celsius)	°F (Fahrenheit)	Gas Mark
Very low	120	250	1
Low	150	300	2
Moderately low	160	325	3
Moderate	180	350	4
Moderately high	190	375	5
High	200	400	6
Very high	230	450	7

BEST SELLERS BY *Nita Mehta*

Different ways with
PANEER

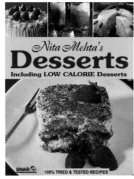

DESSERTS
Including Low Calorie Desserts

FOOD from around
the **WORLD**

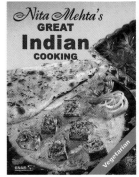

Great
INDIAN Cooking

EVERYDAY
Cooking

QUICK
Vegetarian Cooking

Multicuisine Cooking

MEXICAN
cooking for the Indian kitchen

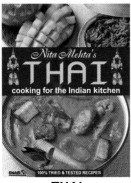

THAI
cooking for the Indian
kitchen

101
MICROWAVE Recipes

VEGETARIAN
Wonders

Perfect Vegetarian
Cookery

Cakes & **Chocolates**

The Art of **Baking**

Soups Salad & Starter

Green Vegetables

Nita Mehta's Children Books

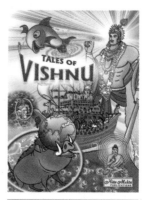

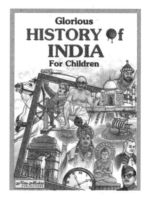